Published by Creative Education
and Creative Paperbacks
P.O. Box 227, Mankato, Minnesota 56002
Creative Education and Creative Paperbacks
are imprints of The Creative Company
www.thecreativecompany.us

Design by The Design Lab
Production by Travis Green
Art direction by Rita Marshall
Printed in the United States of America

Photographs by Alamy (imageBROKER), Biosphoto
(Pierre Huguet-Dubief), Corbis (167/Roy Toft/Ocean,
Vincent Grafhorst/Minden Pictures, Thomas Marent/
Minden Pictures, Pete Oxford/Nature Picture Library),
Dreamstime (Hitman1111, Isselee, Oleksandr Mel-
nyk, Yuriy Zelenen'kyy), Shutterstock (Jessica Bethke,
Natali Glado), SuperStock (FLPA/FLPA)

Library of Congress Cataloging-in-Publication Data
Bodden, Valerie.
Chameleons / Valerie Bodden.
p. cm. — (Amazing animals)
Summary: A basic exploration of the appearance, be-
havior, and habitat of chameleons, the color-changing
reptiles. Also included is a story from folklore explain-
ing why chameleons shake while they walk.
ISBN 978-1-60818-609-9 (hardcover)
ISBN 978-1-62832-215-6 (pbk)
ISBN 978-1-56660-656-1 (eBook)
1. Chameleons—Juvenile literature. I. Title. II. Series:
Amazing animals.
QL666.L23B63 2016
597.95'6—dc23   2014048702

CCSS: RI.1.1, 2, 4, 5, 6, 7; RI.2.2, 5, 6, 7, 10;
RI.3.1, 5, 7, 8; RF.1.1, 3, 4; RF.2.3, 4

HC 9 8 7 6 5
PBK 9 8 7 6 5

CHAMELEONS

BY VALERIE BODDEN

CREATIVE EDUCATION • CREATIVE PAPERBACKS

Some chameleons have a ridge on their heads like a helmet

Chameleons are lizards that can change colors. All lizards are **reptiles**. There are more than 150 kinds of chameleons in the world. And more are still being discovered!

reptiles animals that have scales and a body that is always as warm or cold as the air around it

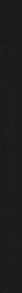

Most chameleons are brown or green. If they are cold, they might get darker. They get brighter when they are angry. Chameleons' eyes stick out from their heads. Each eye can move separately. Most chameleons have bumps or spikes on their backs.

Panther chameleons display a wide range of skin colors

The smallest chameleons are shorter than your thumb. But the biggest chameleons can grow up to 27 inches (68.6 cm) long. Some chameleons' tails are as long as their bodies. They use their tails for balance and to grip branches.

Chameleons' toes face forwards and backwards

Desert chameleons use their color to hide and stay cool

Most chameleons live in Africa. Many are found in **rainforests**. But some live on **mountains** or in grasslands. A few kinds of chameleons even live in hot, dry deserts.

mountains very big hills made of rock

rainforests forests with many trees and lots of rain

Small chameleons eat mites and ants. Larger chameleons gobble beetles, frogs, and even mice. To get water, the lizards lick raindrops off leaves.

Many chameleons feed mostly on insects and worms

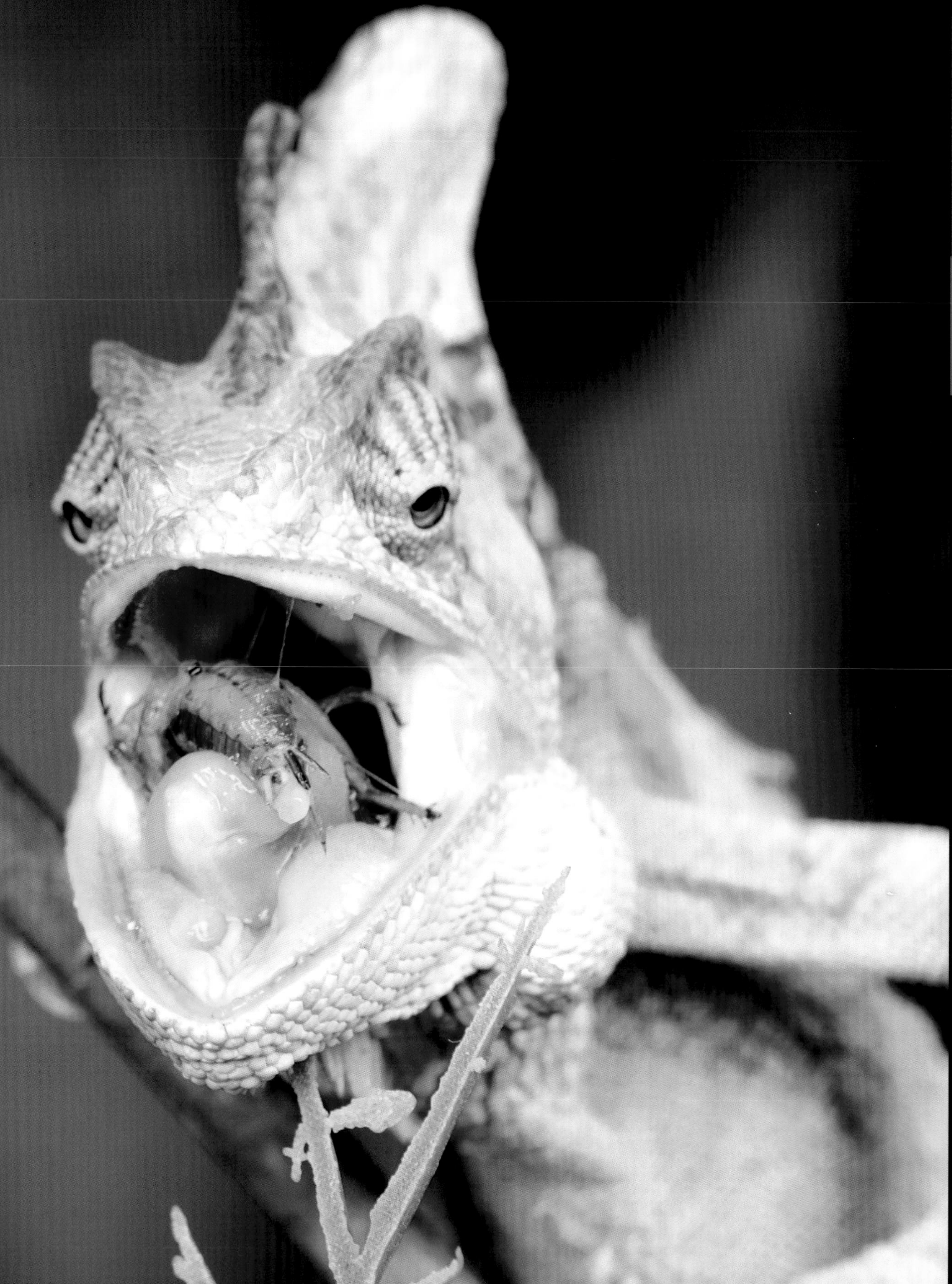

Chameleons usually come out of their eggs in about 4 to 12 months

Most baby chameleons **hatch** from eggs. Mother chameleons do not take care of the babies. Young chameleons shed their skin to get bigger. Most chameleons live about six years. But big kinds of chameleons can live up to 12 years.

hatch come out of an egg

Chameleons spend

their days alone. Each chameleon has its own territory, or living space. Male chameleons sometimes fight over territory.

An angry chameleon puffs up its body and opens its mouth

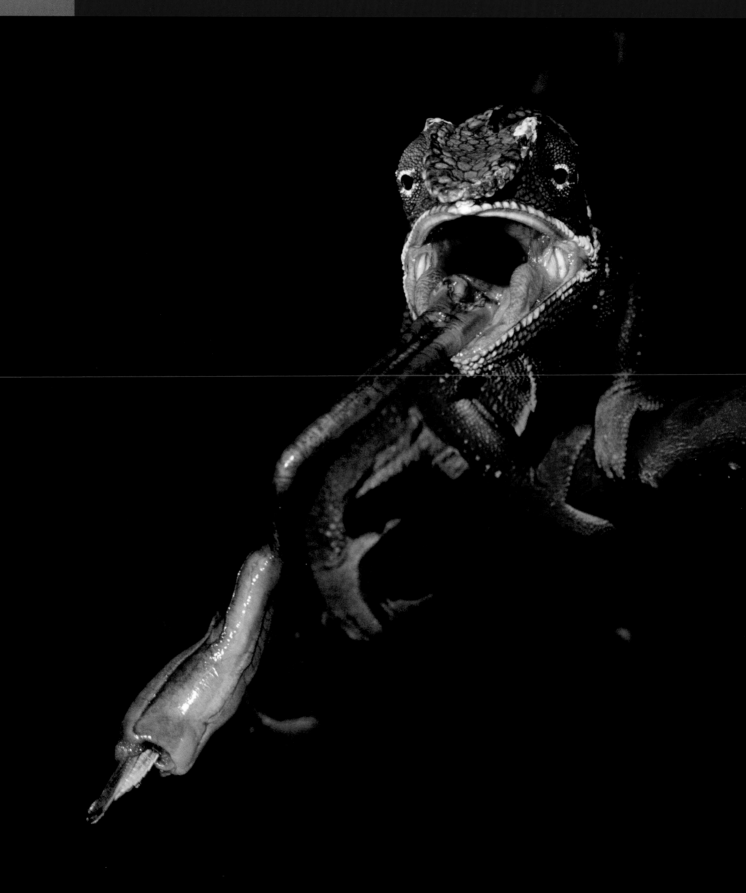

Some chameleons' tongues are longer than their entire body

A chameleon sways back and forth as it walks. This makes it look like a leaf blowing in the wind. Then the chameleon sits on a tree branch and waits for **prey**. When it comes near, the chameleon's long tongue springs from its mouth. A suction cup at the end of the tongue grabs the prey.

prey animals that are killed and eaten by other animals

Some people keep chameleons as pets. Other people go to see them at zoos. These color-changing animals are lots of fun to watch!

Parson's chameleon is one of the largest in the world

A Chameleon Story

Why do chameleons shake when they walk? People in Africa told a story about this. One day, Chameleon helped Spider and Lizard cross the river. He lay down in the water. Spider and Lizard sat on him. As they floated down the river, Chameleon hit a rock. It hurt! From then on, Chameleon walked slowly and tried to shake away the pain.

Read More

Raum, Elizabeth. *Chameleons*. Mankato, Minn.: Amicus, 2015.

Schuetz, Kari. *Chameleons*. Minneapolis: Bellwether Media, 2014.

Websites

Enchanted Learning: Veiled Chameleon
*http://www.enchantedlearning.com/subjects/reptiles/lizard
/Veiledchameleon.shtml*
This site has chameleon facts and a picture to color.

Kids Love Animals: Chameleon
http://www.kids-love-animals.com/?p=1
Watch a video of baby chameleons hatching.

Note: Every effort has been made to ensure that the websites listed above are suitable for children, that they have educational value, and that they contain no inappropriate material. However, because of the nature of the Internet, it is impossible to guarantee that these sites will remain active indefinitely or that their contents will not be altered.

Index

Africa 11, 22
color-changing 4, 7, 20
eggs 15
eyes 7
kinds 4, 11, 15
prey 12, 19
size 8
tails 8
territory 16
tongue 19
young 15
zoos 20